better together*

* This book is best read together, grownup and kid.

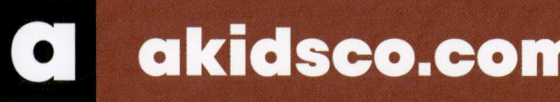

a kids book about COURAGE

by Tasneem Halloum

A Kids Co.
Editor Jennifer Goldstein and Emma Wolf
Designer Rick DeLucco
Creative Director Rick DeLucco
Studio Manager Kenya Feldes
Sales Director Melanie Wilkins
Head of Books Jennifer Goldstein
CEO and Founder Jelani Memory

DK
Delhi Technical Team Bimlesh Tiwary Pushpak Tyagi, Rakesh Kumar
Senior Production Editor Jennifer Murray
Senior Production Controller Louise Minihane
Senior Acquisitions Editor Katy Flint
Acquisitions Project Editor Sara Forster
Managing Art Editor Vicky Short
Managing Director, Licensing Mark Searle

First American edition, 2025
Published in the United States by DK Publishing, 1745 Broadway, 20th Floor,
New York, NY 10019

First published in Great Britain in 2025 by
Dorling Kindersley Limited, 20 Vauxhall Bridge Road, London SW1V 2SA
A Penguin Random House Company

The authorised representative in the EEA is
Dorling Kindersley Verlag GmbH. Arnulfstr. 124, 80636 Munich, Germany

A catalog record for this book is available from the Library of Congress.
A CIP catalogue record for this book is available from the British Library.
ISBN: 978-0-2417-4374-4

DK books are available at special discounts when purchased in bulk for sales
promotions, premiums, fund-raising, or education use. For details, contact:
DK Publishing Special Markets, 1745 Broadway, 20th Floor, New York, NY 10019
SpecialSales@dk.com

Printed and bound in China
www.dk.com
akidsco.com

This book was made with Forest
Stewardship Council™ certified
paper – one small step in DK's
commitment to a sustainable future.
**Learn more at www.dk.com/uk/
information/sustainability**

To my beloved mother, grandmother,
and family, whose resilience, grace,
and love has shown me the
profound essence of courage.

To my beloved sons, Yousef and Zakaria,
whose brave spirit and infinite love have
inspired me to embrace courage,
just as you do.

This book is a humble tribute to the children
of Palestine for their courage, bravery,
and resilience. May this book comfort
your heart and remind you that courage
is within you and has no bounds.

Intro
for grownups

As a mother of 2 extraordinary boys and an educator of exceptional kids, I have seen firsthand the powerful treasure kids hold within them. Over time, this power emerges as one of their greatest strengths, empowering them to face life's challenges with unwavering determination. This is the power of courage.

Courage is often dormant within each of us, waiting to be discovered. Its importance lies in shaping a kid's mindset by fostering resilience, promoting adaptability, strengthening self-belief, and inspiring a positive outlook toward challenges and growth. By guiding our kids to the realization that courage is an innate part of their being and can appear in many forms, we give them the tools they need when they encounter a new challenge or adventure.

Through this book, I hope to help kids discover their courage in all of its forms, empowering them through their journey of life.

HAVE YOU EVER SET OUT
TO DO SOMETHING
(IT DOESN"T MATTER WHAT)
AND FELT AFRAID TO BEGIN?

OR MAYBE YOU CAME FACE-TO-FACE WITH YOUR BIGGEST FEAR AND DIDN"T KNOW WHAT TO DO NEXT.

HAVE YOU EVER FELT STUCK AND UNSURE OF HOW TO GET MOVING AGAIN?

HAVE YOU EVER WANTED TO SAY SOMETHING, BUT FELT YOUR VOICE WOULD FAIL?

What if I told you about a mighty force within you that can help you in any scary moment, tricky situation, or impossible challenge?

I WANT TO SHARE A SECRET

(that really isn't a secret)
about an inner strength
you have deep within you.

A power you can use whenever
you encounter a challenge, set out
on an adventure, or try to do
something really tough.

The secret power is
already inside of you...
AND IT"S CAL

LED COURAGE.

Courage gives you the power to try new things, get through hard times, or stand up for what is right.

Courage comes in many
forms, like being...

BRAVE STRONG BOL

➡ RESILIENT CON

PATIENT ⟳ SILLY

ADAPTABLE ACCOUN

HUMBLE ✤ FLEXI

VULNERABLE ➡

D NOBLE STEADFAST
FIDENT ★ HONEST
COMPASSIONATE
TABLE RESPONSIBLE
BLE ♥ ACCEPTING
TOTALLY, 100% YOU!

At times, you might feel afraid, uncertain, nervous, anxious, shaky, or like you want to throw up.

THAT'S NORMAL! And that's what courage is for! You can feel all those scary feelings and still have courage.

Courage empowers
you to be the best

under any
circumstance.

Sometimes you'll need
courage when things are good

—REALLY GOOD.

Sometimes you'll need
courage when things are rotten

—REALLY ROTTEN.

And sometimes you can share courage with others who need it, because no matter how much courage you use, there is always more inside you!

As a teacher who works with kids (just like you) from all over the world, I can tell you that each and every kid has courage.

COURAGE CAN BE BIG, LIKE MOVING TO A NEW PLACE.

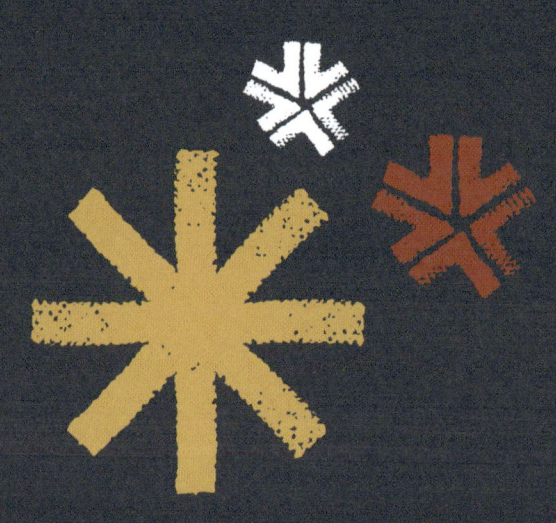

COURAGE CAN BE SMALL, LIKE TRYING SOMETHING NEW.

COURAGE CAN BE LOUD, LIKE STANDING UP TO WORDS AND ACTIONS THAT ARE MEAN OR HURTFUL.

COURAGE CAN BE QUIET, LIKE LETTING GO OF YOUR OWN IDEAS WHEN YOU LEARN A BETTER WAY.

COURAGE CAN BE LONG, LIKE BEING PATIENT.

COURAGE CAN BE SHORT, LIKE A GREAT BIG SMILE.

COURAGE CAN BE HIDDEN, LIKE OVERCOMING THOUGHTS OR WORRIES.

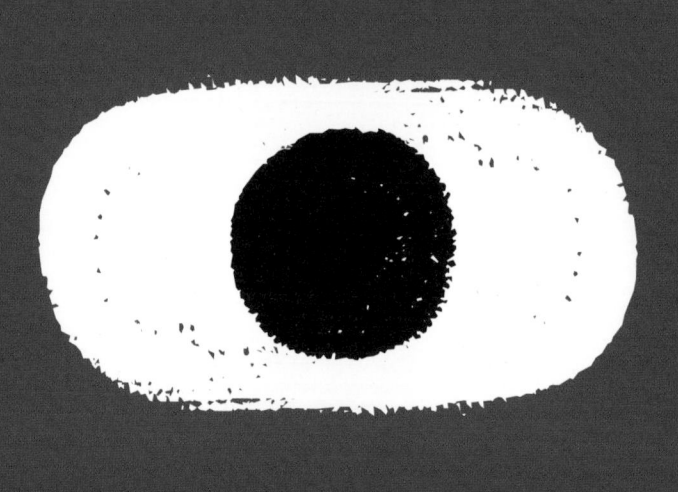

COURAGE CAN BE VISIBLE, LIKE HELPING OTHERS IN NEED.

COURAGE CAN BE STRONG,
LIKE TRYING ONE MORE TIME.

COURAGE CAN BE GENTLE, LIKE A HUG.

COURAGE gives you the power to love yourself, even if you are different from those around you.

COURAGE gives you the power to feel proud of who you are and where you come from while also accepting and appreciating those around you.

COURAGE gives you the power to do what is right and stand up for the truth, even if it seems like you're the only one.

COURAGE gives you the power to be yourself, even if others want you to be different.

COURAGE gives you the power to believe in yourself no matter what.

COURAGE gives you the power to make time to heal and rest.

COURAGE gives you the power to have compassion and kindness even if you are angry, sad, or upset.

COURAGE gives you the power to have patience and forgiveness for yourself and others.

COURAGE gives you the power to be honest with yourself and with others by acknowledging and learning from your mistakes.

COURAGE gives you the power to learn and try something new, even if that means letting go of what is familiar to you.

COURAGE gives you the power to follow your heart and pursue your dreams, goals, and passion.

COURAGE gives you the power to take a stand and make a positive change that makes
the world a better place.

COURAGE gives you the power to help others who are in trouble or need support.

COURAGE gives you the power to tackle challenges, overcome obstacles, and keep going no matter how tough things get.

Sometimes it might seem that courage isn't important, that things would be easier if everything just stayed the same.

BUT THAT WOULD JUST MEAN STAYING STUCK IN THE SAME PLACE.

When we let courage lead us, we can take a different path which guides us to a new adventure.

Sometimes, that's a new flavor of ice cream, and other times, that's sliding down a big water slide.

And sometimes, it's something really big, like knowing when to walk away.

And one of the very best
things about courage is...

YOU ALREA

DY HAVE IT..

It's like your heart beating in your chest.

We don't always remember it's there, but when we do, we can feel it, strong and steady.

So, whether it's the darkest of nights or the brightest of days, the courage within you gives you the power to embrace the adventure of life and be totally,

100%, YOU.

Outro
for grownups

Discovering the courage within is an essential part of our lives. It empowers us to believe in ourselves and have a growth mindset toward any challenge life presents. Courage can come in many forms, big or small, strong or subtle, loud or quiet, and can appear on our good days or not-so-good days.

Grownup, this is an opportunity for you to have meaningful conversation with your kid, exchange experiences, and shed light on the power of courage that is already within them. Praise their courageous efforts, in all forms, no matter the outcome. Learning to recognize the courage within shifts our mindset and gives kids the power to move through life confidently, resiliently, and courageously.

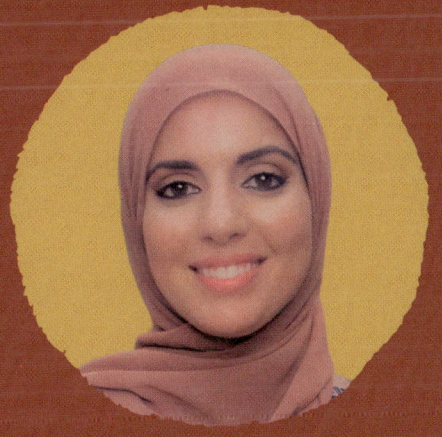

About The Author

Tasneem Halloum is deeply committed to fostering a generation of strong, confident, and compassionate children. As an educator, she has worked with children from diverse backgrounds worldwide, established youth leadership programs in her local community, and is an advocate for educational equity.

Tasneem has learned as much from her children and students as they have learned from her—the most important lesson being on courage. Which is one of the reasons why she wrote this book.

Beyond her passion for education, she finds solace in the pages of books, the beauty of nature, and the joys of an active lifestyle. Most treasured, however, is the time she spends with her beloved children and family.

Made to empower.

a kids book about **racism**
by Jelani Memory

a kids book about ANXIETY
by Ross Szabo

a kids book about DISABILITY
by Kristine Napper

a kids book about IMAGINATION
by LEVAR BURTON

a kids book about belonging
by Kevin Carroll

a kids book about failyure
by Dr. Laymon Hicks

a kids book about GRATITUDE
by Ben Kenyon

a kids book about LIFE ONLINE
by Dave S. Anderson & Blake Fleischacker

a kids book about body image
by Rebecca Alexander

a kids book about IMMIGRATION
by MJ Calderon

a kids book about EMPATHY
by Daron K. Roberts

a kids book about GENDER
by Dale Mueller

a kids book about Love
by ZIGGY MARLEY

a kids book about EQUALITY
by BILLIE JEAN KING

a kids book about MONEY
by Adam Stramwasser

a kids book about FEMINISM
by Emma McIlroy

a kids book about adventure
by Dr. Ben Tertin

a kids book about CLIMATE CHANGE
by Zanagee Artis & Olivia Greenspan

a kids book about CONFIDENCE
by Joy Cho

a kids book about BEING NONBINARY
by Hunter Chinn-Raicht
in partnership with The GenderCool Project

Discover more at akidsco.com